PIANO • VOCAL • GUITAR

THE DEFINITIVE
BROADWAY
COLLECTION

120 Songs

ISBN 0-88188-984-9

HAL•LEONARD®
CORPORATION
7777 W. BLUEMOUND RD. P.O. BOX 13819 MILWAUKEE, WI 53213

Visit Hal Leonard Online at
www.halleonard.com

THE DEFINITIVE
BROADWAY
COLLECTION

All I Ask of You
from THE PHANTOM OF THE OPERA

Music by ANDREW LLOYD WEBBER
Lyrics by CHARLES HART
Additional Lyrics by RICHARD STILGOE

No more talk of dark-ness, for-get these wide-eyed fears: I'm

here, noth-ing can harm you, my words will warm and calm you.

Let me be your free-dom, let day-light dry your tears: I'm

ANOTHER OP'NIN', ANOTHER SHOW

from KISS ME, KATE

Words and Music by
COLE PORTER

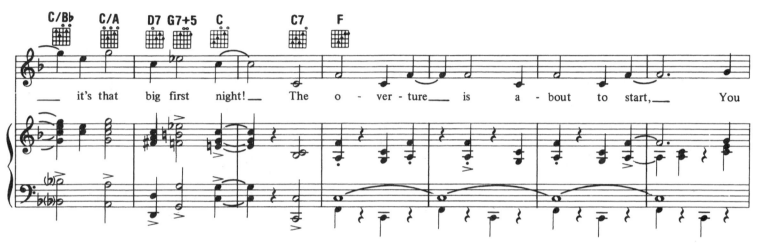

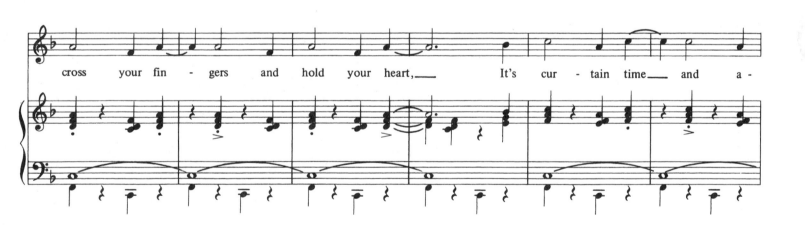

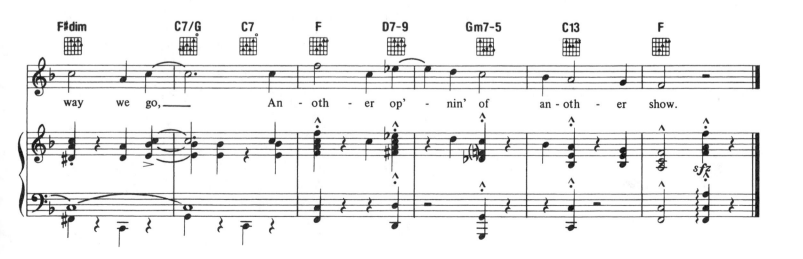

ALL THE THINGS YOU ARE

from VERY WARM FOR MAY

Lyrics by OSCAR HAMMERSTEIN II
Music by JEROME KERN

Some - day my hap - py arms will hold you, and

some - day I'll know that mo - ment di - vine when

all the things you are, are mine!

mine!

AND ALL THAT JAZZ

from CHICAGO

Words by FRED EBB
Music by JOHN KANDER

Moderately

Come on, babe, _ why don't we paint the town, _ and all that jazz! _ I'm gon-na rouge my knees _ and roll my stock-ings down _ and all that jazz! _ Start the car, _ I know a whoop-ee spot _ where the gin is cold _ but the pi-an-o's hot. _ It's just a

bun - ny hug, _ I bought some as - pi - rin _ down at U - nit - ed Drug _ In case we shake a - part _ and want a

brand new start _ to do that jazz! _____

Oh, _____ I'm gon - na see my She - ba shim - my shake. _ (And all that jazz!) _

Oh, _____ she's gon - na shim - my till her gar - ters break. _ (And all that jazz!) _ Show _____

ANTHEM

from CHESS

Words and Music by BENNY ANDERSSON,
TIM RICE and BJORN ULVAEUS

No man, no mad-ness, though their sad pow-er may pre-vail, can poss-

-ess, con-quer my coun-try's heart, they rise to fail.

APPLAUSE

from the Broadway Musical APPLAUSE

Lyric by LEE ADAMS
Music by CHARLES STROUSE

With a Rock Beat

What is it that we're liv-ing for?

Ap-plause, Ap-plause!___ Noth-ing I know___

brings on the glow ___ like sweet ap-plause.___

Being Alive

from COMPANY

Words and Music by
STEPHEN SONDHEIM

AS LONG AS HE NEEDS ME

from the Broadway Musical OLIVER!

Words and Music by
LIONEL BART

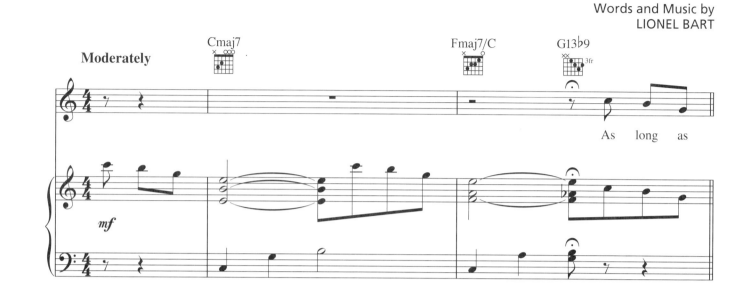

BAUBLES, BANGLES AND BEADS

from KISMET

Words and Music by ROBERT WRIGHT
and GEORGE FORREST
(Music Based on Themes of A. BORODIN)

THE BEST OF TIMES

from LA CAGE AUX FOLLES

Music and Lyric by
JERRY HERMAN

The best of times is now. ___

What's left of sum-mer but a fad-ed rose? ___

CABARET
from the Musical CABARET

Words by FRED EBB
Music by JOHN KANDER

BEWITCHED

from PAL JOEY

Words by LORENZ HART
Music by RICHARD RODGERS

*He's a fool and don't I know it,
**After one whole quart of brandy

But a fool can have his charms; I'm in love and don't I show it,
Like a daisy I awake, With no Bromo Seltzer handy

Like a babe in arms. Love's the same old sad sensation,
I don't even shake, Men are not a new sensation.

* *Standard lyric (in italics)*
** *Original show lyric.*

CAMELOT
from CAMELOT

Words by ALAN JAY LERNER
Music by FREDERICK LOEWE

55

56

CAN'T HELP LOVIN' DAT MAN

from SHOW BOAT

Lyrics by OSCAR HAMMERSTEIN II
Music by JEROME KERN

Slowly

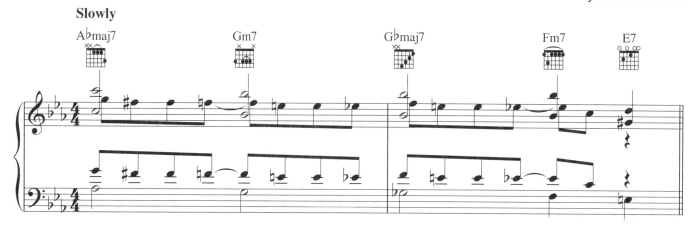

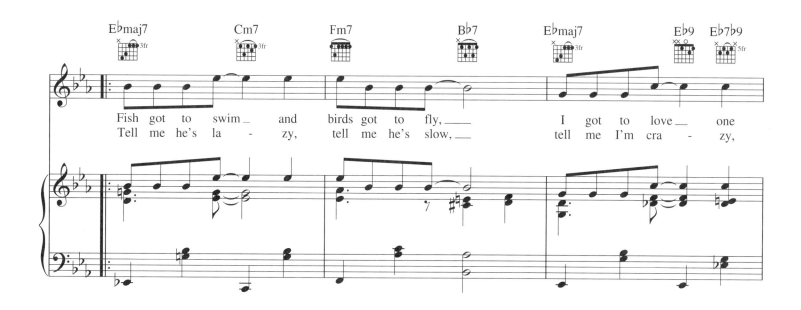

Fish got to swim ___ and birds got to fly, ___ I got to love ___ one

Tell me he's la - zy, tell me he's slow, ___ tell me I'm cra - zy,

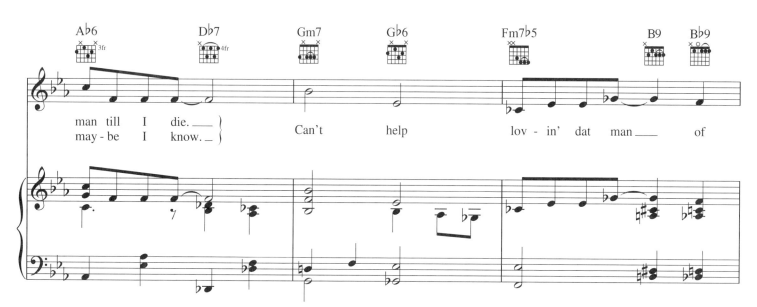

man till I die. ___ }

may - be I know. ___ }

Can't help lov - in' dat man ___ of

CLIMB EV'RY MOUNTAIN
from THE SOUND OF MUSIC

Lyrics by OSCAR HAMMERSTEIN II
Music by RICHARD RODGERS

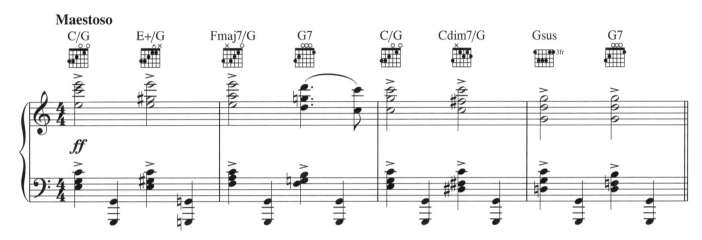

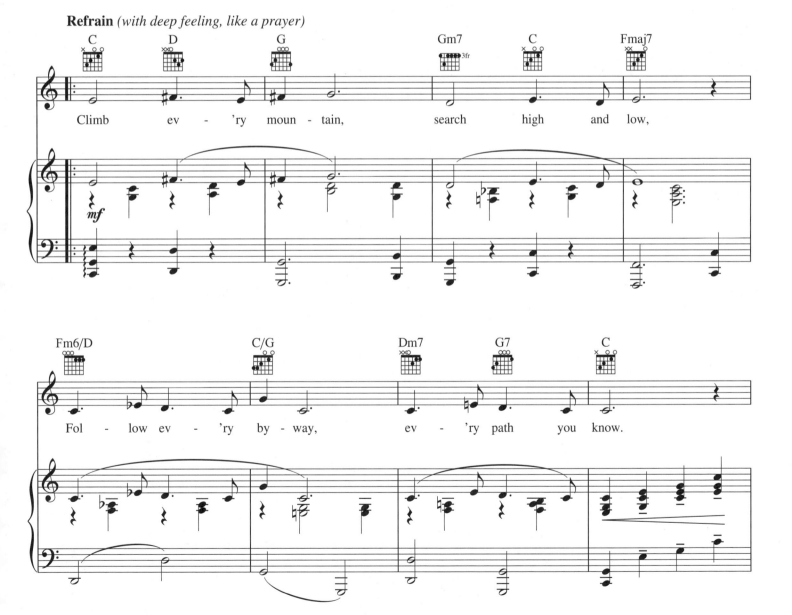

CLOSE EVERY DOOR

from JOSEPH AND THE AMAZING TECHNICOLOR® DREAMCOAT

Music by ANDREW LLOYD WEBBER
Lyrics by TIM RICE

COMEDY TONIGHT

from A FUNNY THING HAPPENED ON THE WAY TO THE FORUM

Words and Music by
STEPHEN SONDHEIM

COME RAIN OR COME SHINE

from ST. LOUIS WOMAN

Words by JOHNNY MERCER
Music by HAROLD ARLEN

CONSIDER YOURSELF

from the Broadway Musical OLIVER!

Words and Music by
LIONEL BART

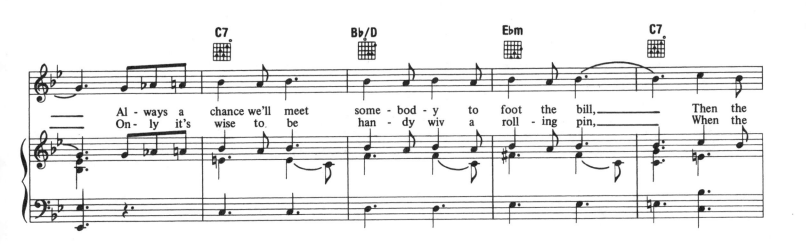

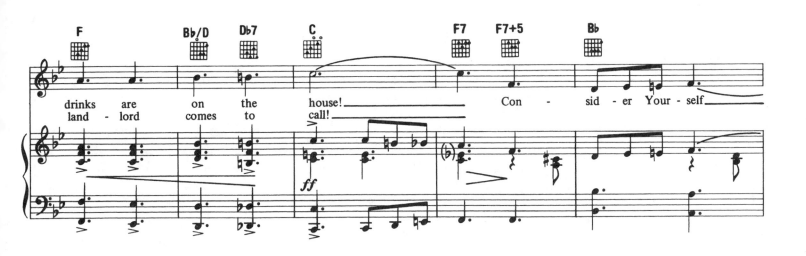

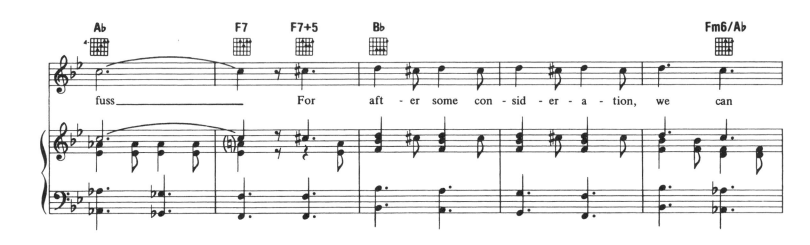

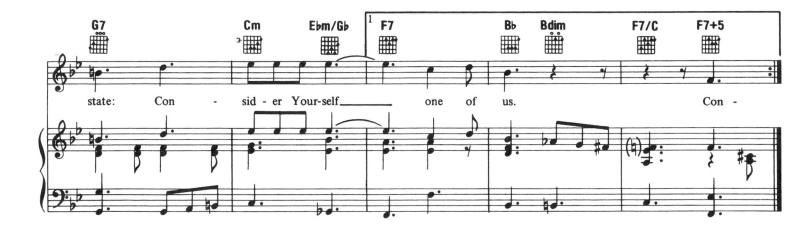

DANCING QUEEN

Words and Music by BENNY ANDERSSON,
BJORN ULVAEUS and STIG ANDERSON

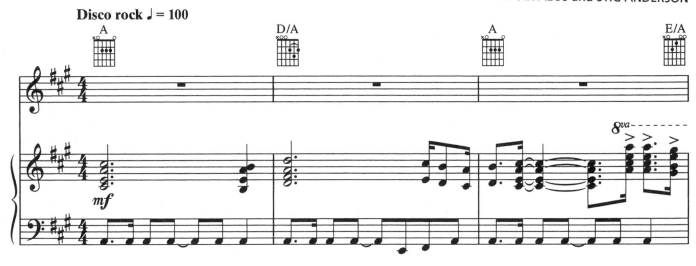

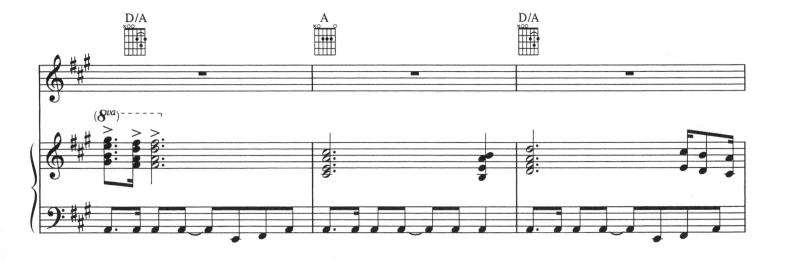

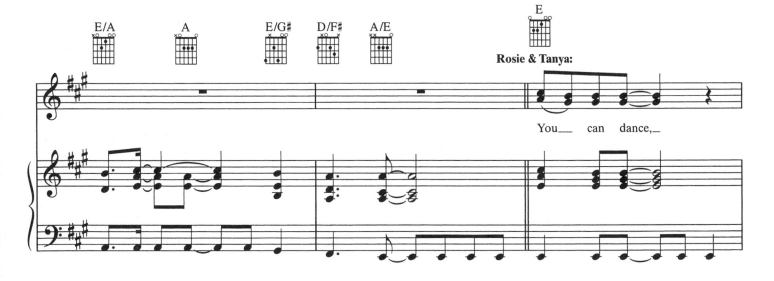

You__ can dance,__

Chorus:

DAY BY DAY
from the Musical GODSPELL

Words and Music by
STEPHEN SCHWARTZ

EDELWEISS
from THE SOUND OF MUSIC

Lyrics by OSCAR HAMMERSTEIN II
Music by RICHARD RODGERS

DO-RE-MI
from THE SOUND OF MUSIC

Lyrics by OSCAR HAMMERSTEIN II
Music by RICHARD RODGERS

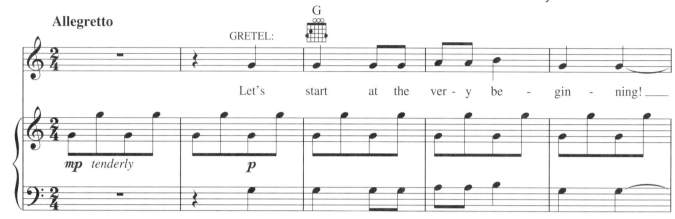

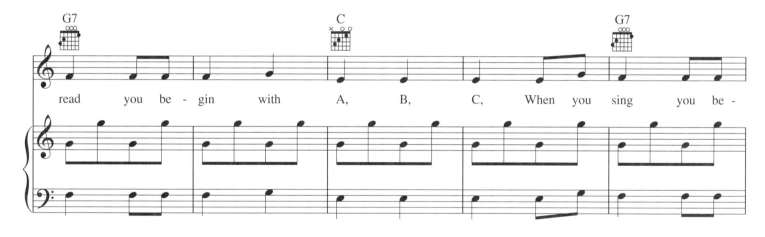

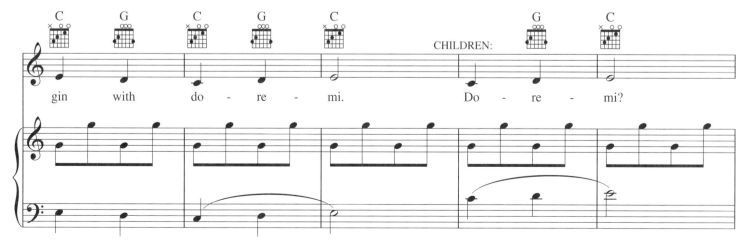

DON'T CRY FOR ME ARGENTINA

from EVITA

Words by TIM RICE
Music by ANDREW LLOYD WEBBER

It won't be ea-sy, you'll think it strange When I try to ex-plain how I feel, That I still need your love af-ter all that I've done: You won't be-lieve me All you will see is a

EVERYTHING'S COMING UP ROSES

from GYPSY

Words by STEPHEN SONDHEIM
Music by JULE STYNE

Lyrics:
Things look swell,_____ Things look great,_____ Gon-na
have the whole world__ on a plate._____ Start-ing here,_____
__ Start-ing now,_____ hon-ey, Ev'-ry-thing's

FROM THIS MOMENT ON

from OUT OF THIS WORLD
from FOSSE

Words and Music by
COLE PORTER

I need so much,_____ Got the skin_____ I

love to touch,_____ Got the arms_____ to

hold me tight,_____ Got the sweet lips__ to

kiss me good - night,_____ From this mo - ment on,___

GET ME TO THE CHURCH ON TIME

from MY FAIR LADY

Words by ALAN JAY LERNER
Music by FREDERICK LOEWE

HELLO, DOLLY!
from HELLO, DOLLY!

Music and Lyric by
JERRY HERMAN

GETTING TO KNOW YOU

from THE KING AND I

Lyrics by OSCAR HAMMERSTEIN II
Music by RICHARD RODGERS

GONNA BUILD A MOUNTAIN

from the Musical Production STOP THE WORLD - I WANT TO GET OFF

Words and Music by LESLIE BRICUSSE
and ANTHONY NEWLEY

Grandioso

grace. With a fine young son

to take my place, I'll leave a

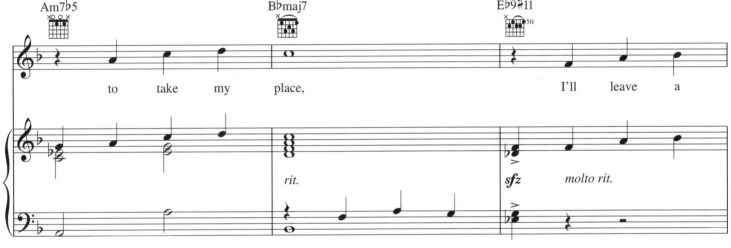

son in my heav-en on earth with the good Lord's grace._____

Extra Verses

Gonna build a heaven from a little hell.
Gonna build a heaven, and I know darn well,
With a fine young son to take my place
There'll be a sun in my heaven on earth
With the good Lord's grace.

Gonna build a mountain from a little hill.
Gonna build a mountain – least I hope I will.
Gonna build a mountain – gonna build it high.
I don't know how I'm gonna do it –
Only know I'm gonna try.

GOODNIGHT, MY SOMEONE

from Meredith Willson's THE MUSIC MAN

By MEREDITH WILLSON

Lyrics:

Good-night, My Some-one, Good-night, my love. Sleep tight, my some-one, sleep tight, my love. Our star is shin-ing its bright-est light For good-night, my love for good-night.___ Sweet dreams be

HELLO, YOUNG LOVERS
from THE KING AND I

Lyrics by OSCAR HAMMERSTEIN II
Music by RICHARD RODGERS

Refrain *(very moderately)*

HOW ARE THINGS IN GLOCCA MORRA

from FINIAN'S RAINBOW

Words by E.Y. HARBURG
Music by BURTON LANE

I CAN HEAR THE BELLS

from HAIRSPRAY

Music by MARC SHAIMAN
Lyrics by MARC SHAIMAN and SCOTT WITTMAN

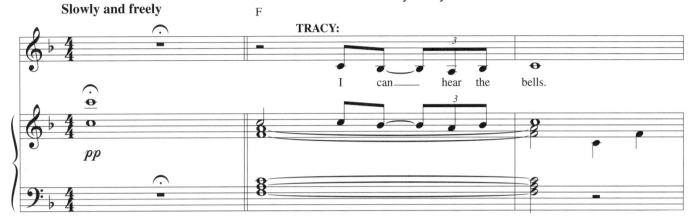

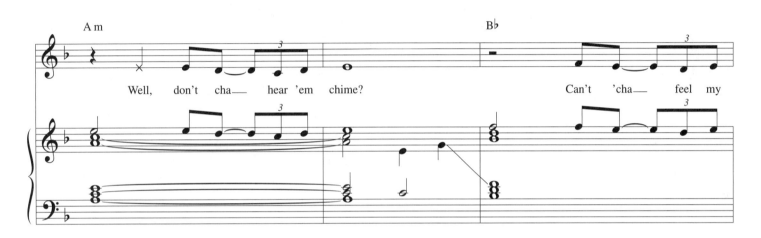

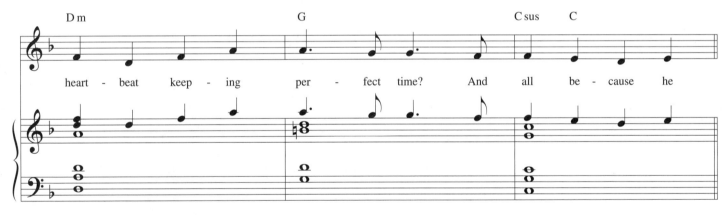

heart was— un-pre-pared when he tapped me and knocked me off my feet.

One lit-tle touch, now my life's com-plete. 'Cause when he nudged me, love

put me— in a fix. Yes, it hit me just like a— ton of bricks. Yes, my

heart burst. Now I know what— life's a-bout. One lit-tle touch and love's

I AIN'T DOWN YET

from THE UNSINKABLE MOLLY BROWN

By MEREDITH WILLSON

I CAN'T GET STARTED WITH YOU

from ZIEGFELD FOLLIES

Words by IRA GERSHWIN
Music by VERNON DUKE

I COULD HAVE DANCED ALL NIGHT

from MY FAIR LADY

Words by ALAN JAY LERNER
Music by FREDERICK LOEWE

I COULD WRITE A BOOK

from PAL JOEY

Words by LORENZ HART
Music by RICHARD RODGERS

I DON'T KNOW HOW TO LOVE HIM

from JESUS CHRIST SUPERSTAR

Words by TIM RICE
Music by ANDREW LLOYD WEBBER

I DREAMED A DREAM

from LES MISÉRABLES

Music by CLAUDE-MICHEL SCHÖNBERG
Lyrics by ALAIN BOUBLIL, JEAN-MARC NATEL
and HERBERT KRETZMER

I WHISTLE A HAPPY TUNE

from THE KING AND I

Lyrics by OSCAR HAMMERSTEIN II
Music by RICHARD RODGERS

I HAVE DREAMED

from THE KING AND I

Lyrics by OSCAR HAMMERSTEIN II
Music by RICHARD RODGERS

I LOVE PARIS

from CAN-CAN
from HIGH SOCIETY

Words and Music by
COLE PORTER

I love Par - is in the win - ter when it driz - zles,

I love Par - is in the sum - mer when it siz - zles.

I love Par - is ev - 'ry mo - ment,_____

ev - 'ry mo - ment of the year._____

I WANNA BE A PRODUCER

from THE PRODUCERS

Music and Lyrics by
MEL BROOKS

LEO & ACCOUNTANTS:

Un - hap - py, un - hap - py, ver - - y un - hap - py, un - hap - py, un - hap - py ver - y, ver - y, ver - y, ver - y, ver - y, ver - y, ver - y, un - hap - py.

SOLO ACCOUNTANT:

Oh, I deb - its all de mor - nin' and I

rit.

colla voce

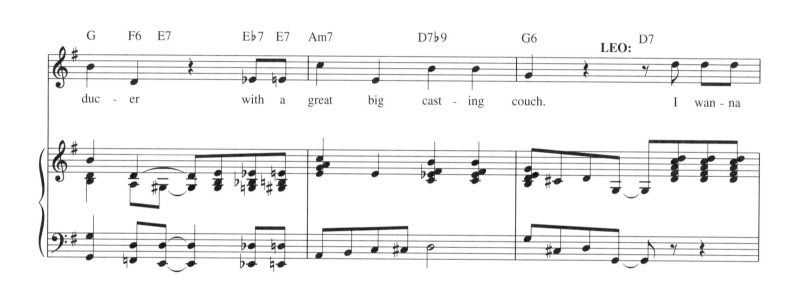

I'VE GROWN ACCUSTOMED TO HER FACE

from MY FAIR LADY

Words by ALAN JAY LERNER
Music by FREDERICK LOEWE

IF EVER I WOULD LEAVE YOU

from CAMELOT

Words by ALAN JAY LERNER
Music by FREDERICK LOEWE

IF I RULED THE WORLD

from PICKWICK

Words by LESLIE BRICUSSE
Music by CYRIL ORNADEL

IF HE WALKED INTO MY LIFE

from MAME

Music and Lyric by
JERRY HERMAN

IF I LOVED YOU

from CAROUSEL

Lyrics by OSCAR HAMMERSTEIN II
Music by RICHARD RODGERS

Allegretto moderato

When I worked in the mill,
Weav-in' at the loom,
I'd gaze ab-sent-
mind-ed at the roof
And half the time the shut-tle 'd
tan-gle in the threads,
And the warp 'd get mixed with the woof

Kind-a scraw-ny and pale,
Pick-in' at my food
And love-sick like
an-y oth-er guy
I'd throw a-way my sweat-er and
dress up like a dude
In a dick-ey and a col-lar and a tie

IF I WERE A BELL

from GUYS AND DOLLS

By FRANK LOESSER

IT MIGHT AS WELL BE SPRING
from STATE FAIR

Lyrics by OSCAR HAMMERSTEIN II
Music by RICHARD RODGERS

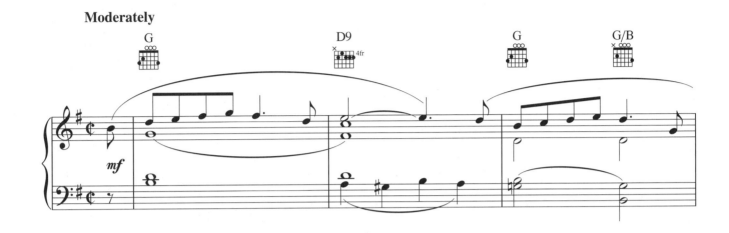

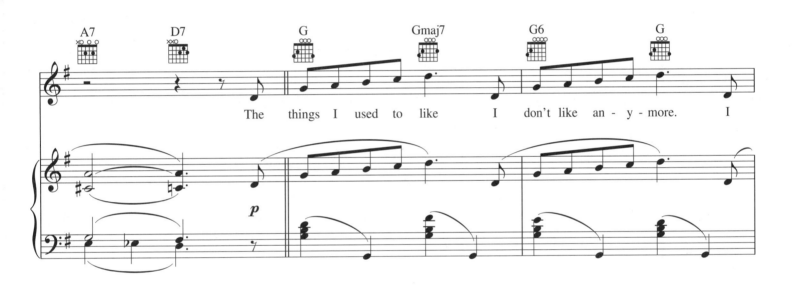

The things I used to like I don't like an-y-more. I

want a lot of oth-er things I've nev-er had be-fore. It's just like moth-er

G/D   Am7   D7   G6   G

says,   I   "sit a - round and   mope"   Pre -

C   Am7♭5   G/D   Am7   D7

tend - ing   I   am   won - der - ful   and   know - ing   I'm   a

G6   G   G6   G   **Refrain** *(gracefully)* G   Gmaj7

dope. _____   I'm   as   rest - less   as   a   wil - low   in   a

p - mf

G   Gmaj7   Dm7   G7

wind - storm,   I'm   as   jump - y   as   a   pup - pet   on   a   string.   I'd

IT'S A GRAND NIGHT FOR SINGING

from STATE FAIR

Lyrics by OSCAR HAMMERSTEIN II
Music by RICHARD RODGERS

Tempo di Valse

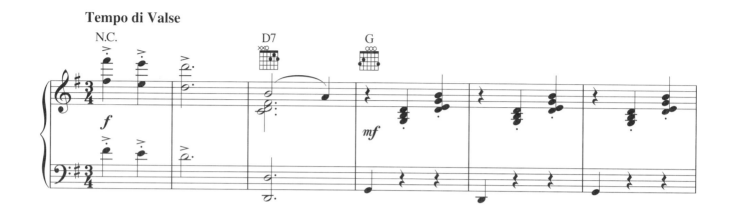

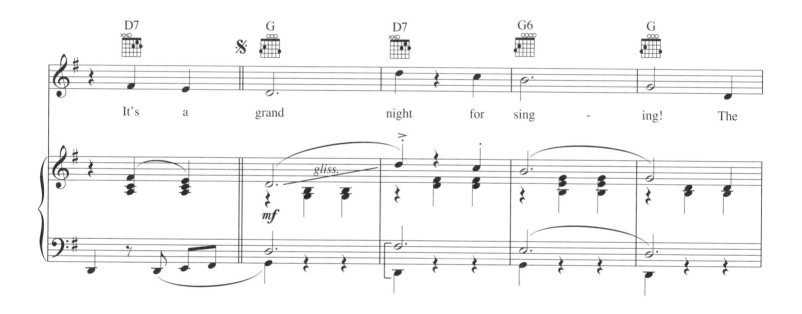

It's a grand night for sing - ing! The

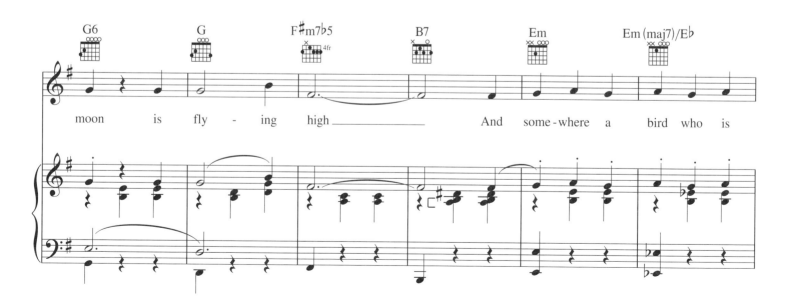

moon is fly - ing high _____ And some - where a bird who is

IT'S DE-LOVELY
from RED, HOT AND BLUE!

Words and Music by
COLE PORTER

*Pronounced "delukes"

JUST IN TIME

from BELLS ARE RINGING

Words by BETTY COMDEN and ADOLPH GREEN
Music by JULE STYNE

KIDS!

from BYE BYE BIRDIE

Lyric by LEE ADAMS
Music by CHARLES STROUSE

THE LADY IS A TRAMP

from BABES IN ARMS
from WORDS AND MUSIC

Words by LORENZ HART
Music by RICHARD RODGERS

LEANING ON A LAMP POST
from ME AND MY GIRL

By NOEL GAY

Moderately, with a lilting swing

Lean - ing on a lamp, may-be you think I took a tramp, or you may think I'm hang-ing 'round to steal a car. _____ But no, I'm not a crook, and if you think that's what I look, I'll tell you

LET ME ENTERTAIN YOU

from GYPSY

Words by STEPHEN SONDHEIM
Music by JULE STYNE

LOOK TO THE RAINBOW

from FINIAN'S RAINBOW

Words by E.Y. HARBURG
Music by BURTON LANE

LOSING MY MIND

from FOLLIES

Words and Music by
STEPHEN SONDHEIM

MAKE BELIEVE

from SHOW BOAT

Lyrics by OSCAR HAMMERSTEIN II
Music by JEROME KERN

MAKE SOMEONE HAPPY

from DO RE MI

Words by BETTY COMDEN
and ADOLPH GREEN
Music by JULE STYNE

MAME

from MAME

Music and Lyric by
JERRY HERMAN

With a lilt

You coax the blues right out of the horn, Mame,___
You've brought the cake-walk back into style, Mame,___

You charm the husk right off of the corn, Mame,___
You make the weep-in' wil-lowtree smile, Mame,___

You've got the ban-joes strum-min' and plunk-in' out a tune to beat the
Your skin is Dix-ie sat-in, there's reb-el in your man-ner and your

MEMORY

from CATS

Music by ANDREW LLOYD WEBBER
Text by TREVOR NUNN after T.S. ELIOT

MY FAVORITE THINGS
from THE SOUND OF MUSIC

Lyrics by OSCAR HAMMERSTEIN II
Music by RICHARD RODGERS

MY FUNNY VALENTINE
from BABES IN ARMS

Words by LORENZ HART
Music by RICHARD RODGERS

OH, WHAT A BEAUTIFUL MORNIN'
from OKLAHOMA!

Lyrics by OSCAR HAMMERSTEIN II
Music by RICHARD RODGERS

Moderate Waltz

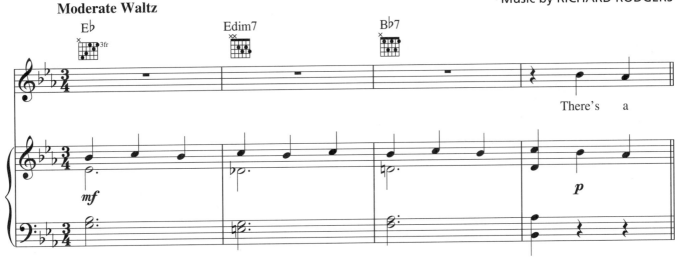

There's a

bright gold - en haze on the mead - ow, _____
cat - tle are stand - in' like stat - ues, _____
sounds of the earth are like mu - sic, _____

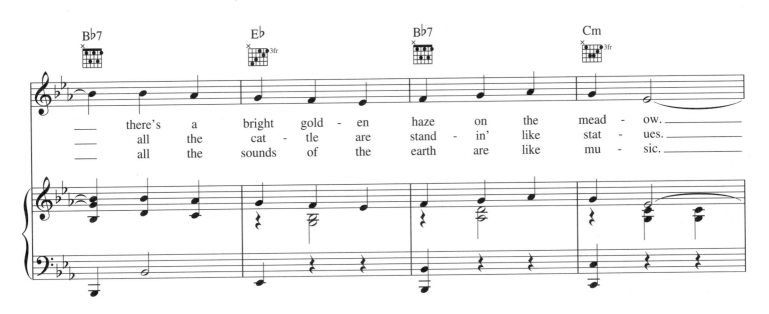

___ there's a bright gold - en haze on the mead - ow. _____
___ all the bright cat - tle are stand - in' like stat - ues. _____
___ all the sounds of the earth are like mu - sic. _____

MY HEART BELONGS TO DADDY

from LEAVE IT TO ME

Words and Music by
COLE PORTER

OKLAHOMA

from OKLAHOMA!

Lyrics by OSCAR HAMMERSTEIN II
Music by RICHARD RODGERS

OLD DEVIL MOON

from FINIAN'S RAINBOW

Words by E.Y. HARBURG
Music by BURTON LANE

ON A CLEAR DAY
(You Can See Forever)
from ON A CLEAR DAY YOU CAN SEE FOREVER

Words by ALAN JAY LERNER
Music by BURTON LANE

ON MY OWN

from LES MISÉRABLES

Music by CLAUDE-MICHEL SCHÖNBERG
Lyrics by ALAIN BOUBLIL, JOHN CAIRD,
TREVOR NUNN, JEAN-MARC NATEL
and HERBERT KRETZMER

Andante

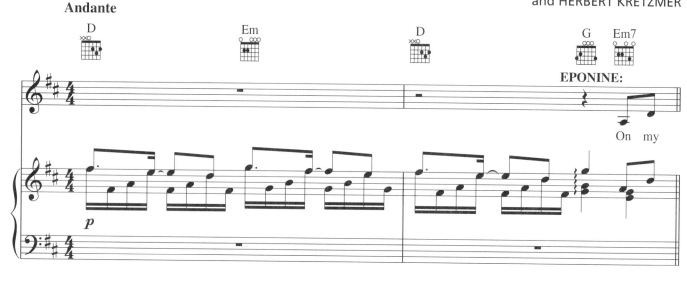

EPONINE:

On my

own, pre-tend-ing he's be-side me. ____ All a-
rain, the pave-ment shines like sil-ver. ____ All the

lone I walk with him 'til morn-ing. With-out
lights are mist-y in the riv-er. In the

ON THE STREET WHERE YOU LIVE

from MY FAIR LADY

Words by ALAN JAY LERNER
Music by FREDERICK LOEWE

ONE DAY MORE

from LES MISÉRABLES

Music by CLAUDE-MICHEL SCHÖNBERG
Lyrics by ALAIN BOUBLIL, JEAN-MARC NATEL
and HERBERT KRETZMER

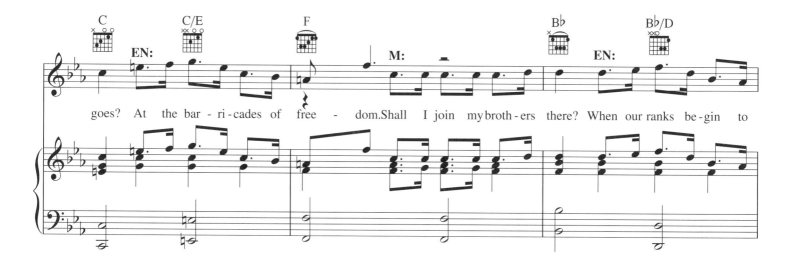

ONE SONG GLORY

from RENT

Words and Music by
JONATHAN LARSON

love. Glo - ry _____ from the soul of a young man, _____

a young man. Find _____

the one song be - fore the vi - rus takes hold, glo - ry

like a sun - set. One song to re - deem _____

THE PARTY'S OVER

from BELLS ARE RINGING

Words by BETTY COMDEN and ADOLPH GREEN
Music by JULE STYNE

PEOPLE
from FUNNY GIRL

Words by BOB MERRILL
Music by JULE STYNE

PEOPLE WILL SAY WE'RE IN LOVE

from OKLAHOMA!

Lyrics by OSCAR HAMMERSTEIN II
Music by RICHARD RODGERS

Moderately

Why do they think up sto-ries that link my name with
Some peo-ple claim that you are to blame as much as

yours? I.
Why do the neigh-bors gos-sip all day, be-
Why do you take the trou-ble to bake my

hind their doors?
fav - 'rite pie?

I know a way to
Grant-in' your wish, I

POPULAR
from WICKED

Music and Lyrics by
STEPHEN SCHWARTZ

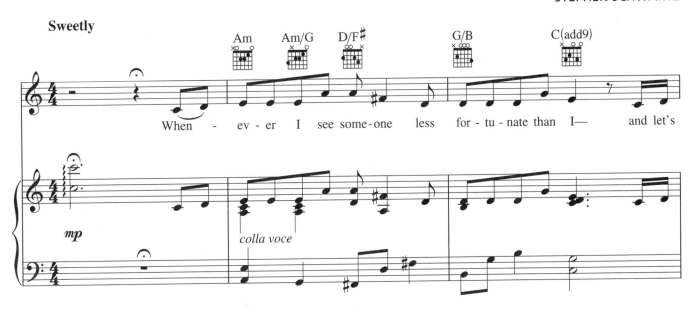

When - ev - er I see some - one less for - tu - nate than I— and let's

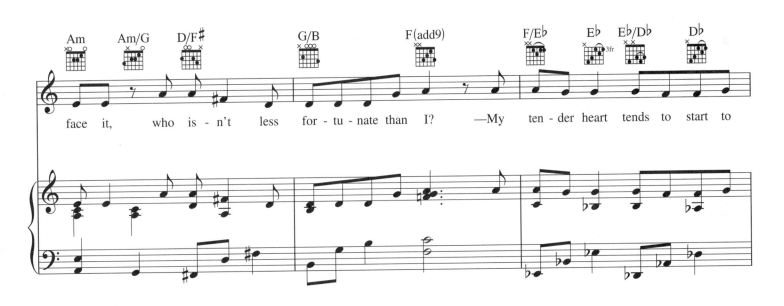

face it, who is - n't less for - tu - nate than I? —My ten - der heart tends to start to

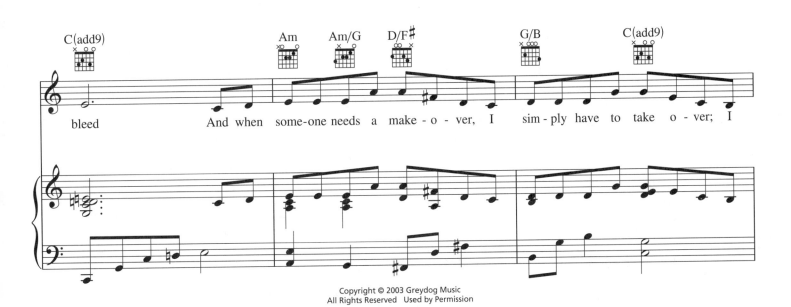

bleed And when some - one needs a make - o - ver, I sim - ply have to take o - ver; I

PUT ON A HAPPY FACE

from BYE BYE BIRDIE

Lyric by LEE ADAMS
Music by CHARLES STROUSE

326

THE RAIN IN SPAIN

from MY FAIR LADY

Words by ALAN JAY LERNER
Music by FREDERICK LOEWE

SEASONS OF LOVE
from RENT

Words and Music by
JONATHAN LARSON

SMOKE GETS IN YOUR EYES

from ROBERTA

Words by OTTO HARBACH
Music by JEROME KERN

Moderately

With pedal

They asked me how I knew my true love was

true. _____ I, of course, re- plied, some- thing here in-

side can- not be de- nied. _____

SEPTEMBER SONG
from the Musical Play KNICKERBOCKER HOLIDAY

Words by MAXWELL ANDERSON
Music by KURT WEILL

SEVENTY SIX TROMBONES
from Meredith Willson's THE MUSIC MAN

By MEREDITH WILLSON

while a hun-dred and ten cor - nets played the air._____

_____ Then I mod-est-ly took my place as the one and on-ly

bass, and I oom - pahed up and down the square._____

Buh buh buh buh buh buh buh buh buh buh buh,_____ Buh buh buh buh buh

SMALL WORLD

from GYPSY

Words by STEPHEN SONDHEIM
Music by JULE STYNE

SOME ENCHANTED EVENING

from SOUTH PACIFIC

Lyrics by OSCAR HAMMERSTEIN II
Music by RICHARD RODGERS

Some en-chant-ed eve-ning ___ You may see a stran-ger, ___

You may see a stran-ger ___ A-cross a

SOMEONE ELSE'S STORY
from CHESS

Words and Music by
BENNY ANDERSSON, TIM RICE
and BJORN ULVAEUS

Slow 8 - Beat Ballad

FLORENCE:

Long a-go _____ in

some-one el-se's life - time, some-one with my name ___ who looked _ a lot _ like me _

came to know _____ a man and made a pro - mise. He on-ly had to say and

SOMEBODY LOVES ME

from GEORGE WHITE'S SCANDALS OF 1924

Words by B.G. DeSYLVA and BALLARD MacDONALD
Music by GEORGE GERSHWIN
French Version by EMELIA RENAUD

When this world be - gan it was Heav - en's plan.

There should be a girl for ev - 'ry sin - gle

man. To my great re - gret

SOMEONE LIKE YOU

from JEKYLL & HYDE

Words by LESLIE BRICUSSE
Music by FRANK WILDHORN

SONG ON THE SAND

(La Da Da Da)
from LA CAGE AUX FOLLES

Music and Lyric by
JERRY HERMAN

Wistfully

Do you re-call that wind-y lit-tle beach we walked a-long? That af-ter-noon in fall, that af-ter-noon we met? A fel-la with a con-cer-ti-na sang; what was the song? It's strange what we re-call, and

THE SOUND OF MUSIC
from THE SOUND OF MUSIC

Lyrics by OSCAR HAMMERSTEIN II
Music by RICHARD RODGERS

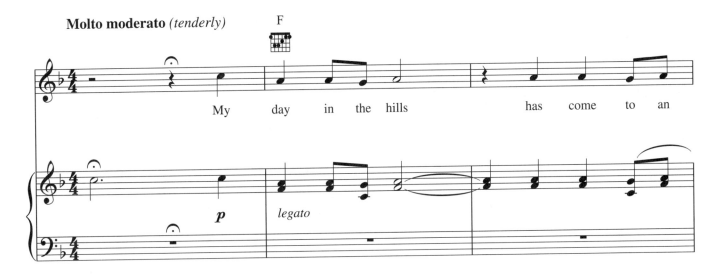

SPEAK LOW

from the Musical Production ONE TOUCH OF VENUS

Words by OGDEN NASH
Music by KURT WEILL

STRANGER IN PARADISE

from KISMET
from TIMBUKTU!

Words and Music by ROBERT WRIGHT
and GEORGE FORREST
(Music Based on Themes of A. BORODIN)

SUPERSTAR

from JESUS CHRIST SUPERSTAR

Words by TIM RICE
Music by ANDREW LLOYD WEBBER

SUPPER TIME

from the Stage Production AS THOUSANDS CHEER

Words and Music by
IRVING BERLIN

THE SURREY WITH THE FRINGE ON TOP

from OKLAHOMA!

Lyrics by OSCAR HAMMERSTEIN II
Music by RICHARD RODGERS

Brightly

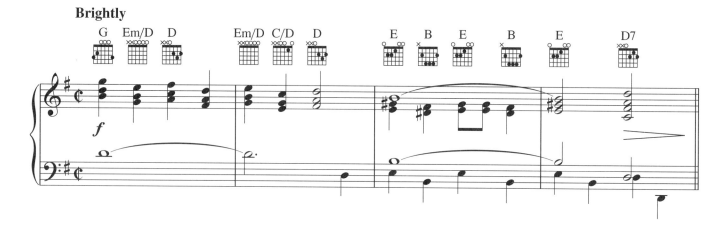

When I take you out, to-night, with me, _____

Hon-ey, here's the way it's goin' to be: _____

fringe on top! Watch that fringe and see how it flut-ters
fringe on top! When we hit that road, hell fer leath-er,
fringe on top! I can feel the day get-tin' old-er,

when I drive them high step-pin' strut-ters, Nos-ey pokes-'ll
cats and dogs-'ll high dance in the heath-er, birds and frogs-'ll
feel a sleep-y head on my shoul-der, nod-din', droop-in'

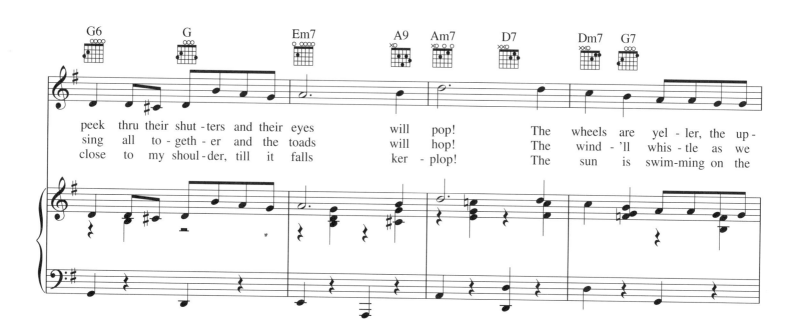

peek thru their shut-ters and their eyes will pop! The wheels are yel-ler, the up-
sing all to-geth-er and the toads will hop! The wind-'ll whis-tle as we
close to my shoul-der, till it falls ker-plop! The sun is swim-ming on the

rig, I'm a - think - in' you c'n keep your rig if you're think - in' 'at I'd
go on for - ev - er? Don't you wisht y'd go on for - ev - er and ud
dream worth a - keep - in', whoa! you team, and jist keep a - creep - in' at a

keer to swap fer that shin - y, lit - tle sur - rey with the fringe on the
nev - er stop in that shin - y, lit - tle sur - rey with the fringe on the
slow clip clop. Don't you hur - ry with the sur - rey with the fringe on the

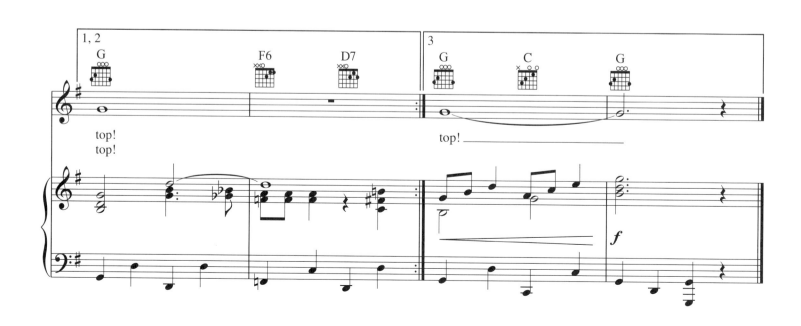

top!
top! top!

TELL ME ON A SUNDAY
from SONG & DANCE

Music by ANDREW LLOYD WEBBER
Lyrics by DON BLACK

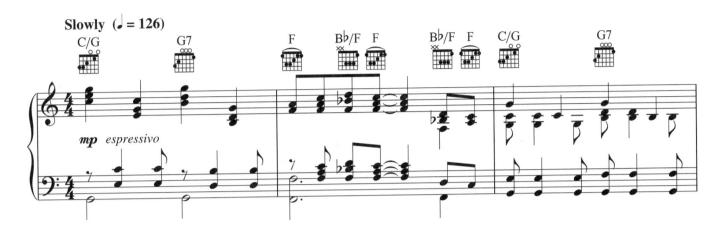

Don't write a let - ter when you want to leave,

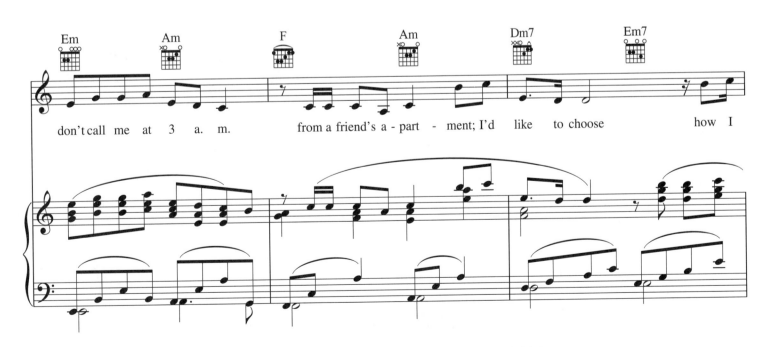

don't call me at 3 a. m. from a friend's a - part - ment; I'd like to choose how I

THE SWEETEST SOUNDS

from NO STRINGS

Lyrics and Music by
RICHARD RODGERS

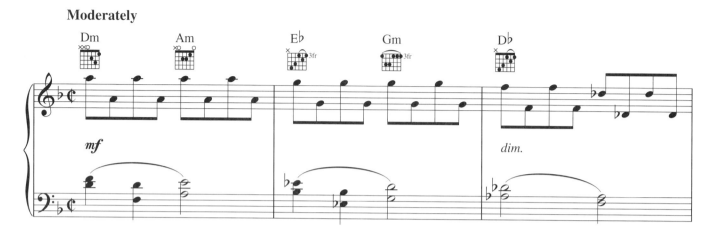

THERE'S A SMALL HOTEL
from ON YOUR TOES

Words by LORENZ HART
Music by RICHARD RODGERS

There's a small ho-tel With a wish-ing well; I wish that we were there to-geth - er. There's a brid-al suite; One room bright and neat, Com -

THIS CAN'T BE LOVE
from THE BOYS FROM SYRACUSE

Words by LORENZ HART
Music by RICHARD RODGERS

THERE'S NO BUSINESS LIKE SHOW BUSINESS

from the Stage Production ANNIE GET YOUR GUN

Words and Music by
IRVING BERLIN

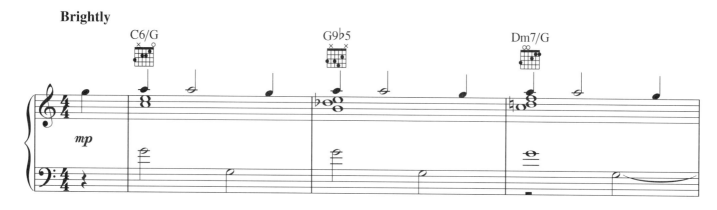

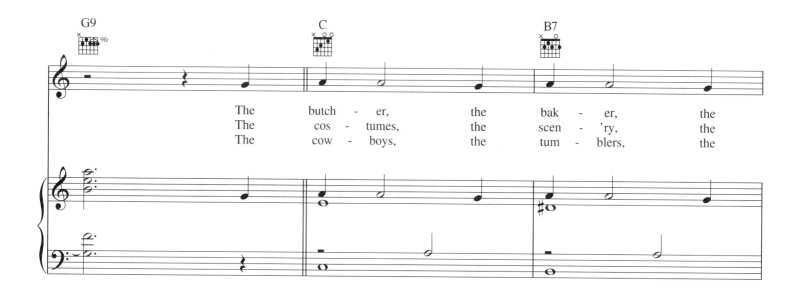

The butch - er, the bak - er, the
The cos - tumes, the scen - 'ry, the
The cow - boys, the tum - blers, the

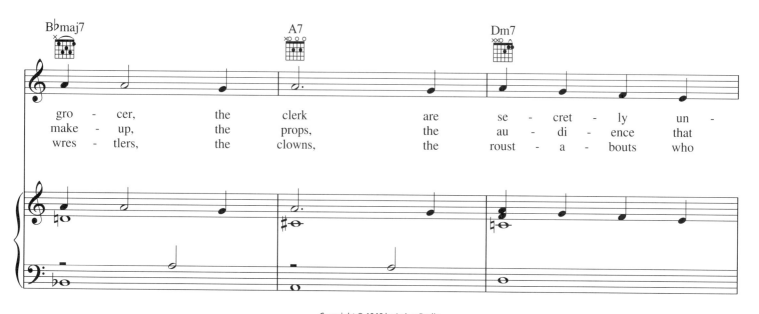

gro - cer, the clerk are se - cret - ly un -
make - up, the props, the au - di - ence that
wres - tlers, the clowns, the roust - a - bouts who

THEY LIVE IN YOU

Disney Presents THE LION KING: THE BROADWAY MUSICAL

Music and Lyrics by MARK MANCINA,
JAY RIFKIN and LEBO M

THIS IS THE MOMENT

from JEKYLL & HYDE

Words by LESLIE BRICUSSE
Music by FRANK WILDHORN

Slowly

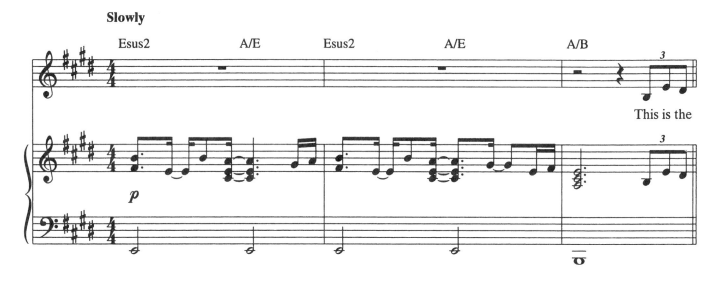

This is the

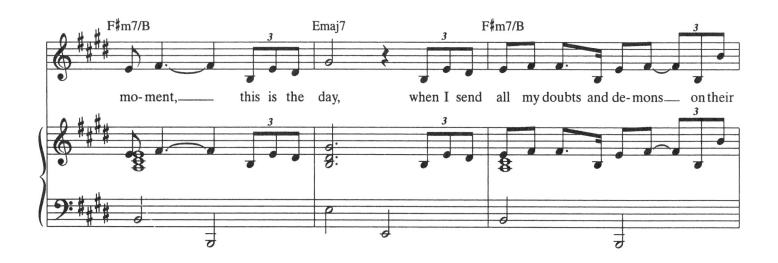

mo- ment,____ this is the day, when I send all my doubts and de- mons____ on their

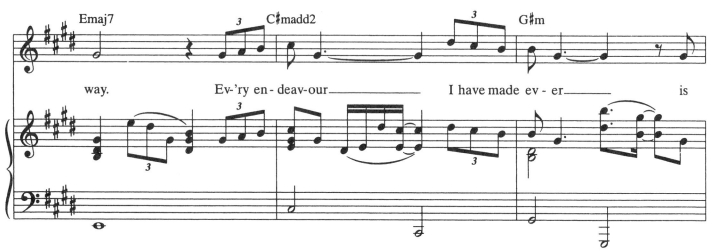

way. Ev-'ry en- deav- our____ I have made ev- er____ is

428

UNEXPECTED SONG
from SONG & DANCE

Music by ANDREW LLOYD WEBBER
Lyrics by DON BLACK

Gently (♩ = 76)

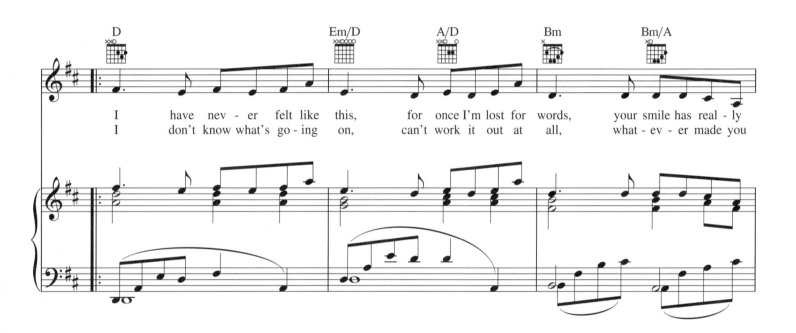

I have nev - er felt like this, for once I'm lost for words, your smile has real - ly
I don't know what's go - ing on, can't work it out at all, what - ev - er made you

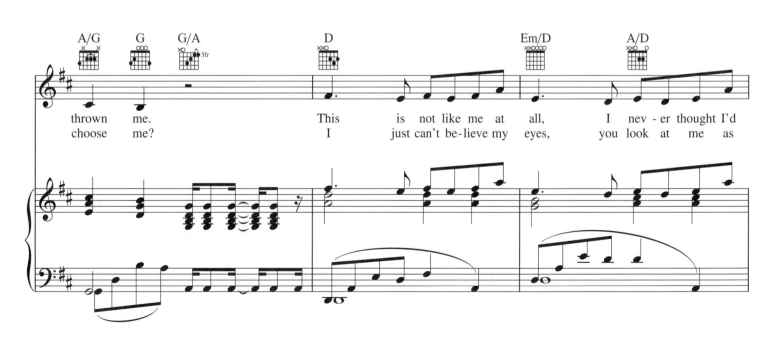

thrown me. This is not like me at all, I nev - er thought I'd
choose me? I just can't be - lieve my eyes, you look at me as

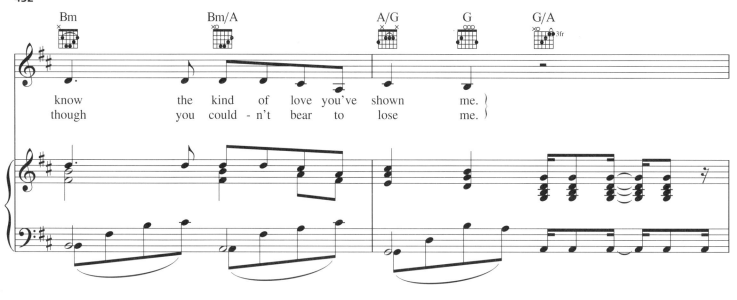

know _____ the kind of love you've shown _____ me.
though _____ you could-n't bear to lose _____ me.

Now, _____ no mat-ter where I am, no mat-ter what I do, _____ I see your face ap-

pear-ing _____ like an un-ex-pect-ed song, an un-ex-pect-ed

all,   I nev - er thought I'd know   the kind of love you've shown   me.

Now,   no mat - ter where I am,   no mat - ter what I do,   I see your face ap -

pear - ing   like an un - ex - pect - ed song,   an un - ex - pect - ed

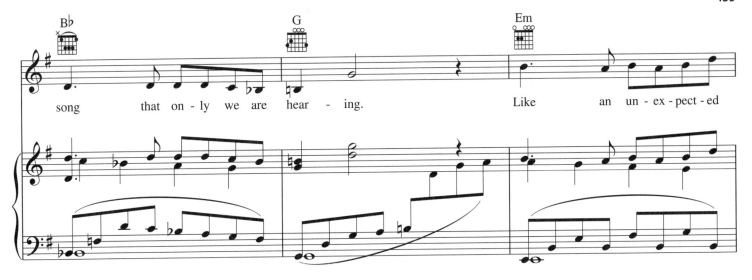

song that on - ly we are hear - ing. Like an un - ex - pect - ed

song, an un - ex - pect - ed song that on - ly we are hear - ing.

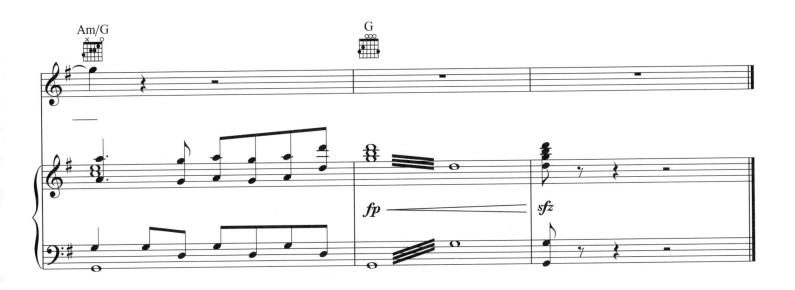

THOU SWELL

from A CONNECTICUT YANKEE
from WORDS AND MUSIC

Words by LORENZ HART
Music by RICHARD RODGERS

TILL THERE WAS YOU
from Meredith Willson's THE MUSIC MAN

By MEREDITH WILLSON

There were bells on the hill, but I never heard them ringing. No, I never heard them at all 'till there was you. There were

birds in the sky, but I never saw them winging, No, I

TOMORROW
from the Musical Production ANNIE

Lyric by MARTIN CHARNIN
Music by CHARLES STROUSE

Moderately slow

The sun - 'll come out _____ to - mor - row, bet your bot - tom dol - lar that to - mor - row _____ there'll be sun! Jus' think - ing a - bout _____ to - mor - row

clears a-way the cob-webs and the sor-row _____ till there's

none. When I'm stuck ___ with a day that's gray and

lone-ly, I just stick ___ out my chin and grin and

say: _____ Oh! the

TRY TO REMEMBER

from THE FANTASTICKS

Words by TOM JONES
Music by HARVEY SCHMIDT

WHAT I DID FOR LOVE
from A CHORUS LINE

Music by MARVIN HAMLISCH
Lyric by EDWARD KLEBAN

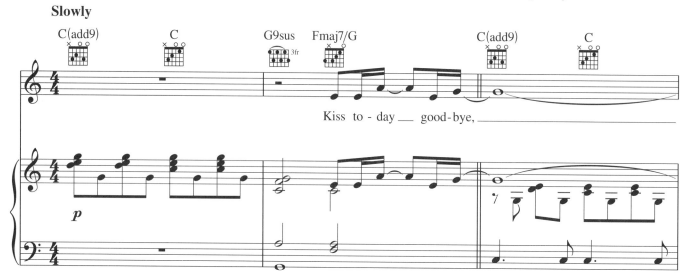

Kiss to-day __ good-bye,

__ the sweet-ness and the sor-row. _____ Wish me luck, _ the

same to you. _____ But I can't re-gret __

WHAT KIND OF FOOL AM I?

from the Musical Production STOP THE WORLD—I WANT TO GET OFF

Words and Music by LESLIE BRICUSSE
and ANTHONY NEWLEY

WHERE OR WHEN
from BABES IN ARMS

Words by LORENZ HART
Music by RICHARD RODGERS

WHO CAN I TURN TO
(When Nobody Needs Me)
from THE ROAR OF THE GREASEPAINT – THE SMELL OF THE CROWD

Words and Music by LESLIE BRICUSSE
and ANTHONY NEWLEY

Slowly, with expression

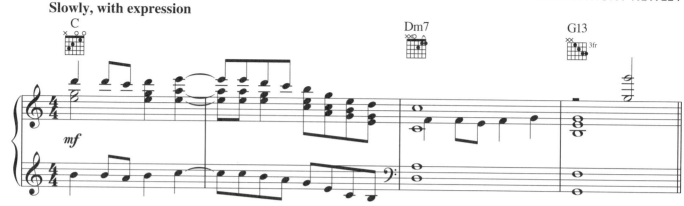

Who can I turn to _____ when no-bod-y needs me? _____ My

heart wants to know and so I must go where des-ti-ny leads me. _____

WHY GOD WHY?
from MISS SAIGON

Music and Lyrics by CLAUDE-MICHEL SCHÖNBERG,
ALAIN BOUBLIL and RICHARD MALTBY JR.

Sostenuto (not too slow)

Why does Sai-gon nev-er sleep at night?_ Why does this girl smell of o-range trees?_

How can I feel good when noth-ing's right?_ Why is she cool when there is no breeze?_ Vi-et-

nam. _____ You don't give an-swers do you, friend?

liked my mem - 'ries as they were, _ but now I'll leave _ re-mem-b'ring her. _

WISHING YOU WERE SOMEHOW HERE AGAIN

from THE PHANTOM OF THE OPERA

Music by ANDREW LLOYD WEBBER
Lyrics by CHARLES HART
Additional Lyrics by RICHARD STILGOE

Andante

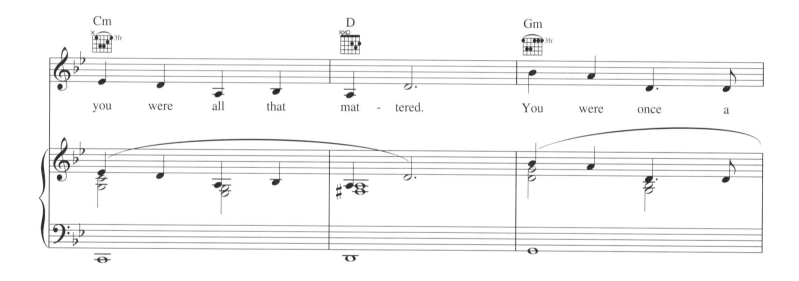

WITH ONE LOOK

from SUNSET BOULEVARD

Music by ANDREW LLOYD WEBBER
Lyrics by DON BLACK and CHRISTOPHER HAMPTON,
with contributions by AMY POWERS

Lento moderato

mp espressivo

NORMA:

With one look I can break your heart, with one look I play ev - ery part. I can make your sad heart sing, with one look you'll know all you need to know. With one smile I'm the girl next door

WOULDN'T IT BE LOVERLY

from MY FAIR LADY

Words by ALAN JAY LERNER
Music by FREDERICK LOEWE

WRITTEN IN THE STARS

from Elton John and Tim Rice's AIDA

Music by ELTON JOHN
Lyrics by TIM RICE

YOUNGER THAN SPRINGTIME

from SOUTH PACIFIC

Lyrics by OSCAR HAMMERSTEIN II
Music by RICHARD RODGERS

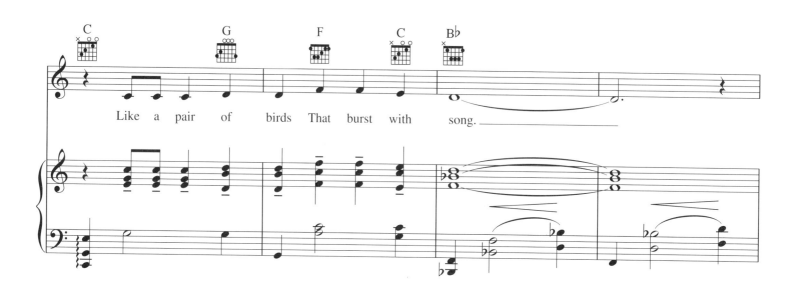

YOU'LL NEVER WALK ALONE
from CAROUSEL

Lyrics by OSCAR HAMMERSTEIN II
Music by RICHARD RODGERS

* alternate lyric: hold your head up high

THE DEFINITIVE COLLECTIONS

These magnificent folios each feature a quintessential selection of songs. Each has outstanding piano/vocal arrangements showcased by beautiful full-color covers. Books are spiral-bound for convenience and longevity.

The Definitive Blues Collection

A massive collection of 96 blues classics. Songs include: Baby, Won't You Please Come Home • Basin Street Blues • Everyday (I Have the Blues) • Gloomy Sunday • I'm a Man • (I'm Your) Hoochie Coochie Man • Milk Cow Blues • Nobody Knows You When You're Down and Out • The Seventh Son • St. Louis Blues • The Thrill Is Gone • and more.
00311563 ....$29.95

The Definitive Broadway Collection

120 of the greatest show tunes ever compiled into one volume, including: All I Ask of You • And All That Jazz • Don't Cry for Me Argentina • Hello, Dolly! • I Could Have Danced All Night • I Dreamed a Dream • Memory • Some Enchanted Evening • The Sound of Music • The Surrey with the Fringe on Top • Tomorrow • What I Did for Love • more.
00359570 ....$29.95

The Definitive Christmas Collection

An authoritative collection of 127 Christmas classics, including: Blue Christmas • The Chipmunk Song • The Christmas Song (Chestnuts Roasting) • Feliz Navidad • Frosty the Snow Man • Happy Hanukkah, My Friend • Happy Holiday • (There's No Place Like) Home for the Holidays • O Come, All Ye Faithful • Rudolph, the Red-Nosed Reindeer • Tennessee Christmas • more!
00311602 ....$24.95

The Definitive Classical Collection

129 selections of favorite classical piano pieces and instrumental and operatic literature transcribed for piano. Features music by Johann Sebastian Bach, Ludwig van Beethoven, Georges Bizet, Johannes Brahms, Frederic Chopin, Claude Debussy, George Frideric Handel, Felix Mendelssohn, Johann Pachelbel, Franz Schubert, Johann Strauss, Jr., Pyotr Il'yich Tchaikovsky, Richard Wagner, and many more!
00310772 ....$29.95

The Definitive Country Collection

A must-own collection of 101 country classics, including: Coward of the County • Crazy • Daddy Sang Bass • Forever and Ever, Amen • Friends in Low Places • God Bless the U.S.A. • Grandpa (Tell Me About the Good Old Days) • Help Me Make It Through the Night • I Was Country When Country Wasn't Cool • I'm Not Lisa • I've Come to Expect It from You • I've Cried My Last Tear for You • Luckenbach, Texas • Make the World Go Away • Mammas Don't Let Your Babies Grow Up to Be Cowboys • Okie from Muskogee • Tennessee Flat Top Box • Through the Years • Where've You Been • and many more.
00311555 ....$29.95

The Definitive Dixieland Collection

73 Dixieland classics, including: Ain't Misbehavin' • Alexander's Ragtime Band • Basin Street Blues • Bill Bailey, Won't You Please Come Home? • Dinah • Do You Know What It Means to Miss New Orleans? • I Ain't Got Nobody • King Porter Stomp • Maple Leaf Rag • Original Dixieland One-Step • When the Saints Go Marching In • and more.
00311575 ....$29.95

The Definitive Hymn Collection

An amazing collection of 218 treasured hymns, including: Abide with Me • All Glory, Laud and Honor • All Things Bright and Beautiful • At the Cross • Battle Hymn of the Republic • Be Thou My Vision • Blessed Assurance • Church in the Wildwood • Higher Ground • How Firm a Foundation • In the Garden • Just As I Am • A Mighty Fortress Is Our God • Nearer, My God, to Thee • The Old Rugged Cross • Rock of Ages • Sweet By and By • Were You There? • and more.
00310773 ....$29.95

The Definitive Jazz Collection

88 of the greatest jazz songs ever, including: Ain't Misbehavin' • All the Things You Are • Birdland • Body and Soul • Girl from Ipanema • The Lady Is a Tramp • Midnight Sun • Moonlight in Vermont • Night and Day • Skylark • Stormy Weather • Sweet Georgia Brown.
00359571 ....$29.95

The Definitive Love Collection

100 sentimental favorites! Includes: All I Ask of You • Can't Help Falling in Love • Endless Love • The Glory of Love • I've Got My Love to Keep Me Warm • Isn't It Romantic? • Love Me Tender • Save the Best for Last • So in Love • Somewhere Out There • Unforgettable • When I Fall in Love • You Are So Beautiful • more.
00311681 ....$24.95

The Definitive Movie Collection

A comprehensive collection of 105 songs that set the moods for movies, including: Alfie • Beauty and the Beast • Blue Velvet • Can You Feel the Love Tonight • Easter Parade • Endless Love • Forrest Gump Suite • Theme from Jurassic Park • My Heart Will Go On • The Rainbow Connection • Someday My Prince Will Come • Under the Sea • Up Where We Belong • and more.
00311705 ....$29.95

The Definitive Rock 'n' Roll Collection

A classic collection of the best songs from the early rock 'n' roll years – 1955-1968. 95 songs, including: Barbara Ann • Chantilly Lace • Dream Lover • Duke of Earl • Earth Angel • Great Balls of Fire • Louie, Louie • Rock Around the Clock • Ruby Baby • Runaway • (Seven Little Girls) Sitting in the Back Seat • Stay • Surfin' U.S.A. • Wild Thing • Woolly Bully • and more.
00490195 ....$29.95

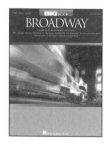